Earth Citizen

Earth *Citizen*

Recovering Our Humanity

ILCHI LEE

**BEST
LIFE**

6560 HIGHWAY 179, STE. 114

SEDONA, AZ 86351

WWW.BESTLIFEMEDIA.COM

1-877-504-1106

FIRST PAPERBACK EDITION: JULY 2009

ISBN: 978-1-935127-25-3

In a sense, each of us is an island. In another sense, however, we are all one. For though islands appear separate, and may even be situated at great distances from one another, they are only extrusions of the same planet, Earth.

—J. Donald Walters

CONTENTS

INTRODUCTION: *A Simple Proposal for Change 9*

CHAPTER 1: *A Big, Beautiful Blue Marble 17*

CHAPTER 2: *A Personal Search for Meaning 25*

CHAPTER 3: *The Persistent Power of Hope 35*

CHAPTER 4: *Earth Citizenship and Earth Management 45*

CHAPTER 5: *You Are Your BOS 53*

CHAPTER 6: *The Great Expanding Universe 61*

APPENDIX I: *Earth Citizens in Action: The One Dollar Enlightenment Project 69*

APPENDIX II: *International Brain Education Association (IBREA) Foundation 75*

A Simple Proposal for Change

People call this era the "information age" for good reason. The world is chock-full of information, and new information is being generated faster than lightning.

If you want to find out what's going wrong in the world, you're in luck. All sorts of books, films, blogs, and other media can tell you all about the world's problems. Pick up a newspaper or flip on the evening news, and you will be bombarded with information from innumerable experts telling you that the biosphere is crumbling, the economy is on thin ice, and our educational system is failing.

This little book is also about information, but it will tell you very little about the world's problems, and it offers little in the way of facts, statistics, or academic expertise. I figure you already know enough about those. Rather, this book is about changing one very simple and basic piece of information about yourself—your citizenship status. Today there are hundreds of different labels of citizenship—American, Canadian, Japanese, Lithuanian, Zimbabwean, Brazilian, and so forth. However, I believe that there is really just one true classification of citizenship—Earth Citizen.

Of course, we can go on having our different governments, separate currencies, and distinct cultures, but these are of no lasting consequence if we cannot first acknowledge the most powerful entity ever known to humankind, the entity that governs the ebb and flow of life—planet Earth itself. Human beings need to acknowledge that their greatest allegiance should belong not to a human-designed government but to the power on which their very existence depends. People must identify themselves as Earth Citizens before any other designation of identity. Through this simple, painless shift in thinking about ourselves and one another, I believe we can make great changes in the world and its destiny.

I am a person who is not satisfied when I hear people resign themselves to the current human condition, chalking it all up to the inevitabilities of "human nature." I think that all of life, including humankind, is either growing and thriving, or declining and dying. To say "Poverty will always exist" or "War is just part of human existence" is to accept and contribute to the decline of humanity. Life is meant to push onward and upward, always evolving to a higher, more well-adapted form. So, too, humanity must evolve upward. To stagnate, to stay stuck in the quagmire of our current habits and beliefs, is to succumb to our own inertia.

That is why for many, many years I have been searching for solutions, for ways to make life on this planet healthier, happier, and more peaceful. But for the most part I am not satisfied with the kinds of solutions I see offered. Pushing another bill through Congress or offering a tidbit of advice for family harmony is helpful, but it is a little like placing a Band-Aid on a gaping wound. These actions are all very well intentioned, but I am more interested in solutions that cut right to the core of the problems of human existence.

But what *is* the root cause of our problems? I believe that all the problems that we currently face begin and end with the human brain. The human brain creates the ideologies and disputes that keep us embroiled in war. It creates the technologies that pollute our atmosphere. It creates the conditions that lead to poverty and hunger. Fortunately, all answers to these problems also lie within the human brain.

This is why, for more than thirty years, I have focused on the workings of the human brain. I am not a neuroscientist, but I have seen firsthand exactly how powerful the human brain can be, and I have been amazed at how people's lives can change when they begin to realize that they have the power to use their brains as they truly wish. Over the years, I have created numerous programs to help people gain this sort of mastery over the workings of their brains. Collectively, these mind-body training techniques are known as Brain Education System Training (BEST), and they are organized into a progressive, five-step educational process. More than one thousand centers offering BEST training now exist all over the world, including in South Korea, Japan, the United States, and Europe. Through these centers, hundreds of thousands of people have changed their lives by changing their brains.

On my journey, I have faced critics who told me, "But the human brain is as it is. You can't really get rid of the greed and violence that are part of what it is." They are right to a degree. There is a dark side to the human mind that cannot be denied. An evolutionary biologist might say that those traits helped us survive, so these things are just part of our genetic makeup. Yet, more and more, research suggests that the brain is a very malleable organ. The brain is not set in the same way that a kidney or a lung is set in a fixed purpose with a fixed sequence of functions. Neuroscientists are now certain that the brain retains a remarkable ability to rewire itself throughout life.

Furthermore, the abilities to show compassion and cooperation are also a universal part of the human brain's capacity. Yes, human beings can be horrible to one another, perhaps even more maniacally cruel and violent than even the most vicious animal. But human beings can also be incredibly kind and generous. In times of crisis, we are capable of demonstrating behaviors that defy a "survival-of-the-fittest" view of human society. Every culture on Earth values the act of putting others before self and kindness before cruelty. And all humans are capable of demonstrating these traits—if and when they choose to do so.

When it comes right down to it, human beings are unique among the world's creatures because of our ability to choose. We are not limited to predetermined instincts and behaviors. We can choose to be selfish or selfless in every moment.

Many of our current global problems may be rooted in the fact that we are choosing self-centered, individualistic modes of being. Too often, we limit our scope of compassion to ourselves and to our immediate family, only occasionally extending it to strangers in our community or nation. It is only the rare individual who considers the wider, global implications of his or her day-to-day character. Many take their current lifestyles for granted and continue with them, even when they seem isolating and stressful. We have been living this way for many generations, so it seems like the most natural way of life, but it is not natural at all. In fact, it is antinatural, disconnecting us from the rest of nature and from one another.

What I am proposing is that we return to our natural selves and to our natural brain state. This requires only two simple changes in the way we view ourselves and the world:

1. We must identify ourselves as Earth Citizens and hold that identity superior to any identity of nationality, race, or religion.

2. We must redefine our professional and cultural lives to focus on the concept of Earth Management by finding ways to fulfill material needs while also honoring the Earth and our common humanity.

In the following chapters, I share my thoughts about how and why I think these simple concepts can help shift the fate of the planet and help return humanity to a healthy, happy, and peaceful state of being. I also share my personal story of coming to an awareness of the nature of life. My hope is that you will read this book and take away a great feeling of hope about the future of humanity, a hope that you will naturally and easily share with others as part of the Earth Citizen movement.

I intend this Earth Citizen movement to be the simplest kind of movement, spread not by complicated philosophical debate or tomes of academic discourse but through individual interaction between people during their everyday lives. To be a part of this movement, you do not need to attend rallies or study obscure philosophers or pass out leaflets on the street corner.

The only effort required to be part of this movement is a simple willingness to see your true identity as a human being completely and irrevocably connected to this amazing planet Earth. You must simply be willing to see yourself as a great and beautiful expression of the marvelous variety of life Earth has given to the cosmos. You must believe that you have a special role in helping bring humanity to its full expression through the individual, day-to-day choices you make. And most importantly, the next time someone asks the simple question, "Who are you?" you must answer in this simple way, with sincerity and conviction:

"I am an Earth Citizen."

CHAPTER 1

A Big, Beautiful Blue Marble

When astronauts first left Earth's atmosphere, they were quite surprised to see the Earth as it is. No one had seen the Earth in its entirety until that moment. They looked back and saw nothing but a round ball floating in a sea of total blackness. They were accustomed to seeing the Earth as it appeared on maps and globes. Of course, they knew intellectually that there would not be distinct black lines demarking the various national boundaries. But this divided conception of Earth was what they knew, a paradigm hammered into their brains since elementary school. To see the Earth as a single, united entity seemed unfamiliar.

As they looked down, there was no way they could distinguish one country from another. It was just one big blue-and-green sphere, which they described as a blue glass marble floating in space.

Bill Anders, one of the first three humans to have left the orbit of Earth, commented, "After all the training and studying we'd done as pilots and engineers to get to the moon safely and get back, [and] as human beings to explore moon orbit, what we really discovered was the planet Earth." Some of the photographs of the Earth taken during these space flights are thought to have helped ignite popular interest in the modern peace and environmental movements. One of these images still emblazons the popular Earth Day flag.

That moment, now more than forty years ago, represented a great leap in the consciousness of humankind. It was the first time a being from Earth stepped away from the planet to see it from a distant perspective. In the development of humanity, this is equivalent to a major step toward growing up—like a child weaned or a bird leaving the nest for the first time.

The entire story of humanity is a maturation story, a coming-of-age tale. You could say that all human history has been a series of awakenings about the realities of the universe, an ever-expanding under-standing of our world and ourselves. These awaken-ings have included gaining awareness of other human cultures living on Earth, great advances in the devel-opment of technology, and amazing discoveries about the way nature works. Every step in our history has been a step away from a limited point of view to a larger, more inclusive point of view. Over time, we have progressed from the tribe to the village to the city to the nation. As our awareness of life expands, so do the boundaries of our personal identity.

Along the way, we have let go of many misconcep-tions about the world around us as we gained knowl-edge and understanding. Now it seems so silly that people once believed that the world was flat, but this was what fit their perception of the world. All the information that came into their senses told them that the world looked flat, so they concluded that it must be flat. It was only after new data were added to this information that people could conceive of the possibility that the world is round.

Our individual maturation stories are the same. When we are infants, we conceive of little beyond our crib and our parents' loving arms. But as we grow, we learn, sometimes painfully, that we are not the only ones who matter. Eventually we learn to share, to be considerate, and to wait our turn.

Humanity has also reached its time to grow up. There are many difficult situations on the planet now. Just as an adolescent must face the complexities of adult life, we must face the complexities of contemporary human existence. And like an adolescent, we must make the choice between childish, self-serving ways and the higher way of compassion and responsibility. For this reason, it is a great time to be human. All the crises we now face are also a blessing; they are the wake-up call that will raise us to the next level of human existence.

But what will this next step in our collective development look like? To survive and thrive, does the human race need to develop a new body through the process of evolution? Do we need to become like the superintelligent alien creatures depicted in the science-fiction novels? Not at all. In fact, we don't have time for the forces of nature to reshape who we are. We need to act now and change now. But where and how will that next phase of growth appear?

I believe that it will happen in the human brain.

Fortunately, we do not need to wait for the process of natural selection to provide us with a whole new brain. We do not need to hope for some advantageous genetic mutation to allow our brains to become even better than they are now. Our brains are extraordinary just the way they are. What we really need is a better way to use our brains. The capacity for greatness—for compassion, creativity, and renewal—already exists within our brains. It is really just a matter of choice.

Thus far, we have primarily used our brains to divide rather than to unite. Through our rational, analytic minds, we look for differences and distinctions between things. To a certain extent, this is useful, allowing us to understand the difference between a raven and a blackbird, or poisonous and edible mushrooms. But unfortunately, we also habitually use our brains to create ideologies and labels that divide humans from one another. We say, "We are Americans, and they are Koreans." And we also create beliefs that separate and divide. "She is a Muslim, he is a Christian, and I am a Buddhist." "He is a Republican. I am a Democrat." We separate and divide, categorize and analyze until it seems like it is just us against the world.

Now the time has come to use our brains to unite with, rather than divide ourselves from, the rest of humanity. This new way to use the brain can begin with a new way to identify the self, an expanded way to understand who we are and where we come from. Looking at humans in terms of arbitrary borders is now passé. To accept or reject others based on ideology or religion is foolish and dangerous. But what, then, is the identity of human beings?

Think of the image of Earth photographed from space. What are the real borders? None of the borders between countries are visible. The only discernible division is between the outer edge of the planet and the beginning of the vast darkness of space. This is the only real limitation on the human species. We have been able to leave Earth's protective atmosphere for short jaunts, but ultimately we are all dependent on the Earth for our sustenance. Perhaps someday we will even transcend Earth's limits through technologies that carry us to live in another place in the galaxy, but that is clearly a long way away. We all depend on the Earth more than the weakest infant depends on his or her mother.

Boundaries, rulers, and names of nations can change, but the Earth is always our home and our source of life. Earth is the only indelible identity we can have. This is why I am suggesting that we expand our identities beyond the limits of nationality and culture to encompass the only identity that is definite and real by identifying ourselves, first and foremost, as Earth Citizens.

CHAPTER 2

A Personal Search for Meaning

Throughout my youth, I was plagued by one simple question: "Who am I?" So often, we answer this question simply with information about our jobs, name, or age. Someone asks, "Who are you?" You might answer, "I am John Smith." But does this really say anything about who you are? After all, you did not come into this world with your name. Who are you *really*? And why did you come to this Earth to live this life into which you were born?

From a very young age, I wondered what this life of mine was really all about. I wondered how we got here and what the point of this human experience really is.

Some of my earliest memories are of time spent lost in my imagination as I gazed into the clouds. I couldn't concentrate on my studies at all because they seemed to offer no answers to the most fundamental questions about life. My teachers thought I was nothing more than an absent-minded dreamer who would never amount to anything.

Even as a little boy I wondered about such things, but it came to a head one day when I was thirteen years old. On a hot summer day, I asked a friend to go swimming with me at a lake near my home. He came with me, but when we got there he didn't want to come in the water because he didn't know how to swim. I mindlessly told him to come in anyway, that swimming was easy. Like any boy his age, he didn't want to be left out of the fun. So when I swam away from shore, he followed. When I was a little way out, I turned around to see how he was doing. I saw him frantically splashing in the water, trying to stay afloat. I swam back as fast as I could, but by the time I had returned, he had already slipped beneath the surface of the water. I dived into the murky water several times before finding him and pulling him to the surface.

I desperately towed him back to shore, but it was too late. His body was blue and lifeless. I shook him and slapped him, but I could not revive him. Not knowing what else to do, I threw him over my shoulder and began to run toward his home. When I got there, I laid my friend's limp body on the ground. His father ran out of the house, but he could not revive his son eiher. I stood there, numbly watching the scene. When it was clear that life would never return to his son's body, the father turned to me and began beating me with his fists on the head and back. I ran away and hid in the woods until my mother came and found me hiding in the darkness.

This event marked the beginning of one of the darkest periods of my life, a time during which I struggled desperately with questions about the meaning and purpose of life on Earth. Throughout high school, I was brooding and dark, convinced that there must be no reason for life, that it is all a random, meaningless accident that only ends in death. Parents told their kids to steer clear of me, believing I was a bad influence. I remember one day pestering my roommate as he was trying to study for an exam.

"What are you doing?" I asked him.

"Studying for the exam. What else would I be doing?" he replied.

"Why?" I responded.

"What do you mean? To get a good grade, of course."

"Why do you want a good grade?"

"To pass the class and get into a good college."

"Why do you want to get into a good college?"

"To have a good life."

"What is the point of a good life?"

By this time, my roommate was becoming per-turbed at my persistence.

"Why are you asking me these things? Your questions are useless to me. All I care about are the questions on this exam," he said.

"Useless?! But aren't these the most important questions of all? Doesn't everything else depend on these questions?"

With that final comment, the boy stormed out of the dorm room to find a better place to study. A few days later, his request for a new roommate was granted.

My interpersonal skills aside, I still believe I was right to ask these questions. I think we all have these questions lurking inside, in the background, but for me they took center stage. I could not concentrate on anything else because basic questions like, "Who am I?" and "What is life about?" haunted me in every moment. I continued to wrestle with these questions until one day I caught a glimpse of where the answer might lie.

After high school, I felt like I was at a dead end in life. Years before, a teacher of mine in elementary school had written on a grade report that I had "no prospects" for the future. Now, as I was entering adulthood, I began to think he was right. I had failed the college entrance exams twice, and I had no thought about what I wanted to do with my life. Then one day, I noticed a pile of trash building up beneath a bridge in my town. I decided to do something about it.

One cartload at a time, I carried all the trash from under the bridge up into the mountains and buried it all in the ground. On top of this makeshift landfill, I planted pumpkin seeds. The pumpkins grew well, nourished by the decomposing trash beneath the soil. I shared the pumpkins with my neighbors, and they were happy, both with the pumpkins and the removal of the trash. I also felt a sense of purpose for the first time in a long time. I was so surprised to see how much good can come even from a pile of trash!

This experience turned my life around. It did not exactly answer the questions that were haunting me, but it certainly changed my perspective on life. Essentially,

I realized that our sense of meaning can come through being of service to others. I finally applied myself to my studies and managed to get into college, eventually graduating with a degree in medical pathology.

This one awakening didn't quite end my questioning, however. I was still nagged by a need to know more about the purpose and meaning of life. I continued through life in the usual way; I got married, held down a job, raised kids, and so forth. Yet the questions never went away. I needed to find out more about the nature of life. I had to find out what this life is all about.

So one day in my early thirties, I decided to go up into the mountains. I promised myself not to come back down until I had found an answer. I was very serious about finding an answer, so much so that I preferred the thought of dying up there to the idea of coming back to live once again without the answers.

I meditated, fasted, and avoided sleep for twenty-one days. I kept asking, "Who am I? Who am I?" At the end of the twenty-one days, I finally got my answer.

One day during deep meditation, my head felt as though it were going to explode. My whole body seemed to be disintegrating, and my life force was dissipating into the air. I was certain that I was dying. But then a clear voice came to me, saying, "Cosmic energy is my energy. My energy is cosmic energy." This, as enigmatic as it may seem, was my answer.

At that moment, I realized that this "I" that I was attempting to define was merely an illusion, that there is no real separation between me and the rest of the world around me. What I perceived as "self" is just another expression of cosmic energy, the energies of heaven and Earth, what in its totality you might call "God." Any separation between my body, the flowers, the sky, and the trees was just a trick of the senses.

What I experienced there on that mountain is commonly referred to in Eastern philosophies as *enlightenment*. I had experienced the oneness spoken of by many sages throughout history. In other words, I then knew without a doubt that I am one and the same with all existence. I then knew tangibly that I am both everything and nothing at the same time. I was at that moment both humbled and empowered beyond my imagination.

This event began the thirty-year quest that culminates here in this Earth Citizen movement. Once I had felt this oneness, I knew that this held the key to peace on the planet. There is nothing new about this message; many peacemakers have been preaching the message "We are one" for centuries. However, I was given one more message in the form of two images that made the need to bring oneness to humanity all the more urgent.

In my meditations on the mountain, I had seen two images of the Earth. One was of a burned and dying planet; the other was of a lush, verdant planet. It was clear to me that these two images represented the choice that human beings had to make. We can continue our destructive course and bring death to the Earth, or we can choose oneness and create the ideal world we have always dreamed of.

This is why I have spent the past thirty-plus years searching for ways to maximize the potential of the human brain. It is only through the human brain that we can ever hope to create the unity that is our birthright. When I was young, I struggled only because there was information in my brain that said there was an "I" that I had to define in relation to the information held in other people's brains. In an instant on that mountaintop, I let go of all of that, discovering that I am one and the same with the stuff of the universe, and thus one and the same with all the world's people and even the Earth itself.

All of the mind-body techniques I have created are meant to help people experience this basic oneness with all things. Along the way, practitioners of these techniques have experienced profound changes in their lives and great healing to their bodies, minds, and spirits.

I believe that it is an error to act as though enlightenment and universal oneness are experiences belonging only to a few elite spiritual masters. In fact, I am a little hesitant to even use the word *enlightenment* because, with all the baggage of religious and spiritual jargon, it connotes something other than what it really is. In reality, enlightenment is something simple and ordinary, something already sitting there in the brain of every man, woman, and child, waiting to be awakened. Our longing for it can be seen in every loving smile and felt in every selfless gesture, and it is written into our countless stories of lost paradises and futuristic utopias.

That is why I am offering the world this simple idea, the Earth Citizen movement. Really, enlightenment is about information. Often people act as though obtaining the correct spiritual information were the key, but really it is as much about the ability to let go of information as the ability to take it in. Enlightened information is information that expands our awareness and breaks down the illusions of separation. The notion that we are Earth Citizens is also just information, but, unlike information that says, "I belong only to one group of people," it says boldly, "I belong to the Earth, and all the world's people are my compatriots."

Someday we may travel beyond the confines of Earth to inhabit other planets in other galaxies. One day, the Earth may seem like only a small town sitting in the middle of the Milky Way. Will we care what country we come from then? Calling yourself an Earth Citizen will be completely natural in that universe.

But until then, we remain completely physically dependent on the Earth, and I suspect that even the space travelers of the future will remain mentally and spiritually dependent on her beautiful blue bounty. Saving the Earth is really saving humanity. Although many species may be lost in the process, life on this planet will continue in some form, no matter what we do. Earth will recover her balance and continue to nurture life. New life forms will evolve and life will go on, no matter how badly we alter her landscape. *We* are the ultimate losers if we cannot transcend our illusionary game of separation.

Let us give future generations the gift of Earth citizenship by first giving it to ourselves.

CHAPTER 3

The Persistent Power of Hope

In the past, people fought over things that were tangible—land, natural resources, and the like. But these days, it seems that people generally fight over things that cannot be touched or seen. People today are more likely to fight over details of religious and spiritual dogma, which are nothing more than beliefs held in the brain. The human mind is the ultimate, limitless space that can be filled up with an endless amount of information. If one person's beliefs about the world are different than another's, there is no reason to think that one is somehow detracting from the other. There is plenty of room for all sorts of perspectives. Yet people commit all sorts of violent acts based on ideology, as if their own beliefs were in danger if someone else believes differently.

The conflicts we have over beliefs are even more absurd when you consider the fact that what one person wants is not really so different from what other people want. The way I see it, there are really only three things that people want: health, happiness, and peace. When we fight over religions or political ideology, we are simply fighting over the ways to get these three basic things. I've often wondered if all the conflicts in the world would stop instantly if only people could see how similar they are to one another. But ironically, we deprive one another and ourselves of health, happiness, and peace by insisting that our way is the only way to get these things.

One of my favorite songs is "From a Distance," a pop ballad sung by Bette Midler. The lyrics speak of how simple our problems would seem if only we could see things from the wide, all-encompassing perspective of God. From that perspective, our intrinsic similarity is clear, and all our differences fade to a blur. The song's lyrics include these lines: "From a distance you look like my friend, / even though we are at war. / From a distance I just cannot comprehend / what all this fighting is for."

To me, this is the epitome of the Earth Citizen mind-set—the ability to get past the perception of differences to see the profound similarities that unite us all. From this perspective, we can make decisions that are best for the planet and future generations of humankind.

You may think that my attitudes are quite Pollyannaish. Plenty of people in the past have had grand utopian dreams that have come to nothing, from Plato's vision in *The Republic* to Buckminster Fuller's technological dreamland. People scoff at such notions for good reason because, in the end, most of these ideas have fell victim to the typical weaknesses of human character, just as easily as any other human endeavor might.

One thing that I do notice, however, is that all people do seem to have a clear and specific image of the way they would like the world to be. The way I see it, all people carry the blueprints for the ideal human society in their hearts, even if they think it is an impossible dream. Very naturally, all people prefer a society based on cooperation and generosity, rather than selfishness and greed. Anthropologists have found this to be true in the most primitive and the most technologically advanced societies alike.

Many people ignore their inner longing to create a better world, however, simply because they have lost hope. They feel that any attempt to create a better world is futile. After all, it is not comfortable to stand up and try to make a difference. It means that you have to stick your neck out and do something differently. I know this intimately because, in the last thirty years that I have been working for peace, I have faced ridicule and opposition beyond what I would have ever imagined. I have come to realize that real change will require real courage because it means letting go of habits and preconceptions that are comfortable to us, even if they are killing us.

In the year 2000, I was invited to deliver a prayer at the opening ceremony of the Millennium World Peace Summit of Religious and Spiritual Leaders in the General Assembly Hall of the United Nations. This is that prayer:

Prayer of Peace

I offer this prayer of peace
Not to the Christian God
Nor to the Buddhist God
Nor to the Islamic God
Nor to the Jewish God
But to the God of all humanity.

For the peace that we wish for
Is not a Christian peace
Nor a Buddhist peace
Nor an Islamic peace
Nor a Jewish peace
But a human peace
For all of us.

I offer this prayer of peace
To the God that lives within all of us
That fills us with happiness and joy
To make us whole
And help us understand life
As an expression of love for all human beings.

For no religion can be better
Than any other religion
For no truth can be truer
Than any other truth
For no nation can be bigger
Than the Earth itself.

Help us all go beyond our small limits
And realize that we are one
That we are all from the Earth.

That we are all Earth humans
Before we are Indians, Koreans, or Americans.

God made the Earth
We humans have to make it prosper
By realizing that we are of the Earth
And not of any nation, race, or religion.
By knowing that we are truly one
In our spiritual heritage.

Let us now apologize to all humanity
For the hurt that religions have caused
So that we can heal the hurt
Let us now promise to one another
To go beyond egotism and competition
To come together as one in God.

I offer this prayer of peace
To you the almighty
To help us find you within all of us
So that we may stand proudly one day before you
As one humanity.
I offer this prayer of peace
With all Earth humans
For a lasting peace on Earth.

U.S. president Barack Obama named his second book well when he called it *The Audacity of Hope*. It really does take audacity to believe that things can and will change. These days, there is a constant flow of negative information that says, "Give up and give in. This is the way it has always been and the way it will always be." Media outlets constantly exploit our vulnerabilities, keeping us locked in patterns of fear-based thinking. Advertisers solidify our destructive patterns of consumption, telling us we need their products to establish our worthiness as human beings.

I am a person who has a lot of hopeful audacity. There are a lot of people through the years who have told me that I should just give up, but I never do. I have spent almost thirty years looking for ways to make the world a better, more peaceful place. I keep going, always looking for answers. Despite all these struggles, I always come back to the notion that peace is really a very simple thing to achieve. It is not a matter of making a whole new society with new laws and customs. Peaceful, sustainable living is really only a matter of people being true to whom they really are inside. But, in this world, it takes a lot of courage to hold onto these simple and basic values.

I suspect that you, too, are a person with a lot of audacity. You are not a person who has given up on the notion of a better world. You are still in touch with that part of you that can believe that a peaceful, healthy planet is possible. For that reason, I invite you to join with me in making this one small change in your self-identification. Please, from now on, when someone asks you who you are, say, "I am an Earth Citizen."

It may seem a little bit cheeky and a little bit odd, but it is simple to do if you have just a tiny bit of courage. Show the world that you have the audacity to make your habits really match what you believe inside. If you want to give more information later, great, but please answer this simple way first. When people ask, "Where are you from?" say simply, "Earth." You can later tell them your job, nationality, and all these other details, too, but please begin with this basic identity of Earth Citizen. Through this simple concept of Earth citizenship, human beings can begin to see their commonality and unity with one another, rather than always focusing on what separates and divides them.

By calling yourself an Earth Citizen, you are declaring to the world that you are someone brimming with hope and determination to make a better world. Through it, you are saying to the world, "I believe in the Earth. I believe in humanity." While you may be perfectly aware that humanity has made grave errors in the past, you also have deep and abiding faith in the goodness that lies at the heart of humanity.

CHAPTER 4

Earth Citizenship and Earth Management

The question remains, "What does it really mean to be an Earth Citizen?" Just like any other form of citizenship, Earth citizenship carries with it certain responsibilities.

I believe that the ultimate responsibility of an Earth Citizen lies in the care of the Earth and of other beings on the planet. Presently, our dominant cultures do not support this because they are largely based on values inconsistent with peaceful, sustainable living.

I cannot be the one to tell you or anyone else what these specific values must be. For many years to come, we must grapple with the various moral and ethical questions that are part of human society. However, I do know that we urgently need to create a culture that will support, rather than detract from, our common humanity. That part of the transformation needs to happen now.

It will take time to create a better world. But the primary responsibility of all Earth Citizens is to work consistently and diligently toward this goal. It means speaking up for what you think is right and for what you believe to be the highest potential of the human spirit. It means having the courage to get out of the rut of habitual thoughts and behaviors, and to encourage others to do the same. Of course, we may disagree about the details along the way, but as we focus on our common humanity and the Earth itself, I believe we can eventually create a world that is truly healthy, happy, and peaceful. It will take effort, but we can do it.

Personally, it helps me to view the process of making a better world as a simple equation:

New Values + New Culture = A New World

The first step is to formulate the new values on which we can all agree. Through these, a new culture and a new world can be born. The people of the world already argue over so many issues. How do we decide what values are important? For the Earth Citizen, only the Earth itself is the final arbiter of value. The minutiae of ethical debate is immaterial. Nations can continue to form their own laws, and ethnic groups can follow whatever traditions they like. The important thing is to keep the Earth itself in full view whenever we are making decisions about our way of life. Keep any religious or political idea that you want, embrace whatever books, paintings, or films that you like, but always ask yourself to consider what the impact of any given thing is on the Earth and its many children. With that sort of consciousness, anything about the culture that needs to change will change naturally, without the need for mandate or coercion.

People today sometimes point to particular aspects of culture to blame for the state of the world. "Violence in the media is the problem," some say. Others might say, "Our educational system is failing." The things we think are the worst problems in the world—gang violence, rape, starvation, and such—are not the real problems. These things are merely symptoms of the problem. The real problem is the deadening of the human spirit, which leads people toward these behaviors.

I believe that the primary reason we have lost our sense of humanity is that we have lost our connection to the Earth. When we lose our humility in relation to the Earth, believing we have "conquered" nature and eliminated our dependence on the Earth, then we also lose humility in relation to one another. From this arrogant standpoint, it is easy to give in to greed and hatred. But in the end, it is all a big lie because we have not outgrown our dependence on the Earth at all; we have merely closed our eyes and ears to it. And if we continue our ecologically destructive patterns, it will be tragically clear just how dependent we are on the natural world.

Even at the beginning of the Industrial Revolution, the American transcendentalist Henry David Thoreau noted the "savage torpor" that was permeating society as it moved out of nature and into the cities. And as we have "progressed," moving from the Industrial Age to the Information Age, we have become accustomed to living even more completely disconnected from the Earth. Thus the first step toward a better culture is a return to a focus on the Earth.

The information age has brought with it a stressful, isolated way of living. However, there is nothing inherently evil about the new technologies that bring information to us at the speed of light. Yes, you could say, for example, that the Internet provides access to a lot of negative information. But what is really important is how we manage information, not the tools we use to retrieve it. Just as the Internet has the potential to spread hate and fear, it also has the potential to unite people to create a better world.

One great thing about the Internet is its ability to make geographic boundaries obsolete. These days, we can have virtual friends all over the world because of it. Of course, we can use this new way to connect to even further solidify our prejudices and closed-mindedness by seeking out only those who support our preexisting beliefs and preconceptions. But ultimately, I think it will allow people to expand and explore their common humanity to a greater degree than before.

Our quality of life, and perhaps even our survival, depends on how we choose to manage ourselves in relation to the technologies we create. In fact, human culture is basically about management. All cultures have the particular traditions, beliefs, and customs that they do because society needs to manage the individuals who make up the larger group according to the values it holds. Every culture has to decide how to manage the needs of individuals in relation to the needs of the larger group.

Until now, all cultures have been managed in such a way as to help ensure the survival of that particular group. Cultures that did not manage themselves well in relation both to the available natural resources and to other people competing for those resources did not survive. This is why individuals identify so strongly with the groups they belong to. The group's survival is their survival.

But this model is clearly no longer serving the interests of humankind. In today's world, the needs of the entire world must be considered. Earth Citizen culture can take many different forms, but basic respect for the Earth and the entirety of humanity must remain at its core.

To demonstrate honor to and appreciation for the Earth, we need a definite paradigm shift from human-centered to Earth-centered management, what I call *Earth Management*.

Right now, human culture primarily focuses on fulfilling bodily needs. This leads to the competition and overconsumption that plague our planet. Earth Management instead shifts the focus to the Earth and our relationship to it. I believe that this focus will also produce a more heart- and spirit-centered culture.

Even after a very high standard of living has been assured, a kind of hoarding mentality remains. Individuals continue to compete and grab for more and more, until most of the wealth is concentrated in the hands of a very few, and the Earth's environment is depleted. This tendency is merely a habit of the human brain, one that was formed in a darker, more difficult time of human history. Because it is a habit that has led to environmental and political crisis, we must commit ourselves to changing the habit, just as we would change any other destructive habit.

Throughout history, the brain has been crucial to human survival. Through it, we have subdued most of the more treacherous aspects of nature, and we have ensured humanity's collective survival. But now all the ingenious methods that have allowed us to thrive— such as agriculture and manufacturing—put us in danger through the pollution and overpopulation that they encourage. Also, the human brain has invented innumerable perspectives that divide people from one another. In this sense, the brain has become a liability.

But within the brain lies amazing potential for greatness. I do not mean to say that a few individuals possess greatness. *Everyone* possesses greatness within his or her brain.

G reat brains are made, not born.

This statement may sound a little strange to you, since we often speak of great people as though they were somehow apart from the rest of humanity. For many years, scientists have preserved and studied the brains of prodigious geniuses and other extremely talented people, hoping to find some anatomical anomaly that would help them explain the individual's special qualities. While some individual characteristics exist as they exist for any brain, there is no clear anatomical difference between the brains of geniuses and those of ordinary people.

The real difference between an ordinary and an extraordinary brain is how the brain is used. Great people *choose* to use their brains in ways that go beyond ordinary human behavior, and thus they achieve greatness.

I would argue that the people we label as geniuses are really just demonstrating more fully functioning, but ordinary, brains. Greatness, in my opinion, is not the result of a congenitally superior brain. All of us have the potential for greatness. The problem is that most of us never really use the full potential of our brains. In fact, I would say that anyone who is not living up to his or her potential for greatness is not normal at all, but is succumbing to a kind of brain disability.

I am not a neurologist or a psychologist, but through many years of observing how people use their brains, I have noticed some distinct tendencies, ways in which people cut themselves off from realizing their true potential. All of these problems are simply the result of habitual ways of thinking and behaving in the world. I call these three brain maladies Information AIDS, Creative Autism, and Addictive Inertia.

One of the most destructive brain problems is **Information AIDS**. In this case, an individual has lost the ability to distinguish between positive and negative information. In the human body, if the immune system is functioning well, the body instantly attacks any invader that threatens its health. Any bacteria or virus that is potentially harmful will be attacked by antibodies and removed from the bloodstream.

Information can behave very much like a virus in the brain, and, like a virus, it can severely weaken the brain. Like a virus, some information is harmful, and other information is harmless. Also, information can be easily passed from host to host, just like a cold or the flu.

For example, if one person tells another a negative piece of information about someone else, you could say that an informational virus has been passed to one host from another. If this second host has an effective informational immune system, then it will not affect him or her very much. However, if the second host has no immunity to negative information, it could develop into a full-blown informational disease that affects the person's ability to love purely and openly.

Much of the dissension in the world stems from an epidemic of Information AIDS. Negative information about those different from ourselves is often the underlying motivation for the conflicts we face. The Earth Citizen concept is meant to serve as a kind of informational immunity booster, helping people to set aside information that creates dissension between people. The worst information virus is the kind that tells people that they are powerless to change themselves or the world. If they have Information AIDS, the virus grows inside them, and they keep giving themselves more and more bad information: "I am not good enough," "I am powerless," "There is nothing I can do."

Information AIDS is not the only brain disability causing problems today. Another one is **Creative Autism**. In this case, people lose the ability to be cooperatively creative with one another. Actually, Creative Autism is really just the result of many years of living with Information AIDS. These individuals have been affected by debilitating information for so long that they have stopped believing in their own creative potential. This is a serious problem, because it is only through creative cooperation that the world can find lasting peace and environmental sustainability.

We are living in an age that will require astonishing creative ability, not just from an elite, talented few, but from everybody. New values, a new culture, and a new world must be created soon, and to give up your right to help create these is to give up your stake in the future and your connection to future generations of human beings. But unfortunately, like autistic children, who cannot connect to those around them, we keep ourselves locked in a world of individualistic preconceptions about how the world works and how the world should be. The Earth Citizen mind-set helps people break out of the bubble to find connection with other human beings.

The condition of Creative Autism is further complicated by the presence of **Addictive Inertia**. In this case, the brain has become addicted to a certain way of living and relating to other people. A fundamental law of physics, the law of inertia, states that an object in motion will resist any change in direction or velocity. Likewise, people become addicted to certain patterns of brain. Like a ball rolling down a hill, they cannot stop themselves, even if they are rolling right toward the cliff.

Many people today are caught in a state of Addictive Inertia. They can see very clearly that their lifestyle is part of a larger environmental and social problem, but they have a hard time changing the direction of that lifestyle. I believe that the only force that can change the inertia of the current global direction is a collective shift in human consciousness. This shift can be like a strong wind that blows the rolling ball off its current, doomed course. It was a certain mind-set that first started the ball rolling in this direction, and it is also a change in mind-set that will help humanity avoid disaster.

Can the simple concept of Earth citizenship really return our brains to a state of health? I believe that it can because it helps us to reboot our BOS, our Brain Operating System. Just as an operating system like Microsoft Windows or Mac OS determines how a computer can be used, your BOS determines how your brain will be used. Certain fundamental beliefs about who you are and your role on this planet are the most influential programming that your brain contains. This programming can affect every other decision or action generated by the brain.

To reset our BOS, we must first acknowledge ourselves as the true and rightful masters of our brains. Our actions and beliefs are the programs we run on our brain, and information is the language that writes the programs. We must recognize our ability to program our brains in accordance with our highest aspirations and ideals. We must exercise our basic right to evaluate the information and thought patterns that we may otherwise take for granted. You can begin by giving yourself very positive information.

By defining yourself as an Earth Citizen, you have chosen BOS programming that is naturally compatible with any other Brain Operating System on the planet. Make sure that any additional programs you place on your BOS support the creative power you hold inside to make a better world. Keep feeding your brain positive information. It may be easy to return to old patterns of thinking, but keep encouraging yourself. Acknowledge your own creative genius. Understand the truth of your greatness, and keep giving yourself messages that support and develop it.

CHAPTER 6

The Great Expanding Universe

You could say that all of existence is about expansion. Astrophysicists tell us that the cosmos itself is constantly expanding. So, too, does our consciousness. As we go through life, our awareness is constantly expanding as we learn and experience more about the nature of the universe.

The expansion of consciousness could also be defined as the expansion of love. You might think of love as the unifying element, the thing that energetically bonds people together. When we are able to love widely and unconditionally, our consciousness will also shine more brightly in the world.

As our ability to love others grows, it radiates outward from us, reaching farther and farther in its ability to touch others. As love grows, it follows this basic pattern of expansion: self→family→country→the world. When we come into the world as infants, selfish interests are our main obsession. We cry when we are hungry or cold, and we think little of the concerns of others. This is not a bad thing. It is perfectly natural and necessary. You must learn to love yourself first, or you have no basis on which to love others.

As we grow older, we learn to love and care for those around us. Perhaps first we learn to love our parents, and then our siblings, and then our teachers and friends. We identify these people with ourselves and begin to care as much for their welfare as our own. Then, our ability to love expands farther outward to encompass our country and our culture, which provide us with a sense of belonging and strength.

The problem is that the outward expansion of love often gets stuck at this point. Few people are able to truly expand their love beyond their specific group identity, such as nationality or ethnicity. Even those who embrace friends of various cultures and ethnicities divide themselves for other reasons, for example, on the basis of spiritual or political standpoint. Almost universally, the human tendency is to favor those who seem similar to us. As our perceptions of difference become solidified, we may begin to see other groups' interests as threats to our own, or we may hold resentments that are magnified over time. Some of the worst human behaviors—such as warfare, genocide, and racism—become easier to justify if divisive information is held in the brain.

The Earth citizenship concept is a simple way to jump over the walls of group identity. It is a reminder that all of the information we use to separate ourselves is just an illusion. I am not so naive as to believe that all quarrels among human beings will end simply because of a common identity. However, I do believe it is an honest designation of identity and a great first step toward rediscovering our common humanity.

Skeptics might argue that conceptions of separate nationality are a normal outgrowth of human nature, that everyone wants to believe, and will fight to prove, that they and their immediate kin are superior to others. But I have the exact opposite view of human nature. People do give in to hate and violence, but I do not believe that this is the human being's natural state.

Everyone comes into this world with a natural ability to love. Watch a very young child, maybe two or three years old, and you may notice how he or she does not differentiate among people based on religion, race, or any other factor. He or she just wants to love and be loved, purely and simply. It is only later (but unfortunately starting at a very young age) that a child learns to judge people based on the notions of good and bad.

This loss of purity and innocence is reflected in the biblical story of the Garden of Eden. Humanity, represented by Adam and Eve, lived happily in perfect peace and harmony, until that fateful day when they ate of the fruit of the Tree of Knowledge of Good and Evil. This story is symbolic of the loss of innocence that we all experience when information infects our brains that allows us to separate, judge, and divide. Just as Adam and Eve were corrupted by their ability to know the difference between good and evil, we too are corrupted by the information that tells us what is "good" and what is "bad." The information tells us what we should love and what we should hate; it is the information that divides us from one another.

Folklore from my native Korea offers a similar story. In that story, all the people of the Earth lived in harmony in a castle named after Mago, the spirit of the Earth. These people drank directly from the milk of the Earth and remained free of material desires.

But one day, a man was unable to get any milk, so he decided to try eating some grapes. The grapes caused his five physical senses to awaken, which brought with them material desires. Other people also tried the grapes, turning away from the milk of the Earth. This caused dissension and mistrust among the inhabitants of Mago Castle, as they fought to get more grapes. Eventually, the inhabitants left the castle and scattered to different parts of the Earth.

Although this story reflects the corrupted nature of humanity, Korean culture also holds the notion that the original heavenly nature of Mago's inhabitants remains in the human heart. We call this the spirit of *hong ik*, which refers to the human desire to widely benefit all humankind, rather than live only for the desires of the individual self.

I believe that the Earth Citizen movement can help individuals recover the hong ik spirit buried within them. It is like taking a step back toward a simpler time when humanity lived as one family and humbly recognized its dependence on the Earth.

In the book *Born to Be Good*, the psychologist Dacher Keltner argues that the need to demonstrate kindness and compassion is built right into our physiology. Contrary to other biologists who focus on concepts such as the selfish gene, he does not think human beings were designed to live "nasty, brutish, and short" lives, as Thomas Hobbes described it. Rather, we humans appear to be hardwired in both body and brain to thrive in ethical, cooperative societies.

So, then, what is stopping us from living according to these higher impulses? Really, it is just habit. We are in the habit of living primarily in search of individual materialistic gratification. Also, many of us are stuck in the habit of returning to negative judgments and emotions, especially about those who are different from ourselves.

I focus on the brain because habits will change when the brain changes. Neuroscientists now know without any doubt that the human brain is capable of dramatic change. This ability is called *neuroplasticity*, and it allows us to rewire our brains to learn new skills and alter our behaviors at any age. When someone has a habit, it simply means that certain pathways in the brain have been used frequently, and thus it is easy to return to habitual behaviors. You might say that the Earth's problems are the result of the current wiring of people's brains. Through Brain Education System Training and the Earth Citizen movement, I hope to help people rewire their brains in a more peaceful way.

It is not easy to get people to change their thinking; first and foremost, they must be willing to do so. I am hopeful, however, that humanity will soon awaken to the urgency of our situation. Really, human beings are no different in that regard than any other living thing on the planet. None of the beauty and variety you see on Earth came about through comfort and easy prosperity. Struggle has always been an important part of the evolutionary process. Everything, from the alligator's scales to the peacock's plumage to the rainbow of colors in human skin, came about in response to some difficulty that past generations faced.

The same is true of human society. All the cultural and technological developments were made to alleviate some unresolved need. As the old saying goes, "Necessity is the mother of invention." When the brain needs to find a way, it finds a way.

Today's world provides a wonderful opportunity for us to find our true greatness. I always tell people to tell themselves, "I am here because the twenty-first century wanted me desperately." People line up to see superheroes save the day in the movies, but the time has come to start thinking of ourselves as superheroes. We are the ones who have to save the Earth, and our superpowers lie in our brains, waiting to be activated.

Earth Citizens in Action:
The One Dollar Enlightenment Project

There are no specific prerequisites for becoming an Earth Citizen. If you can acknowledge your dependence on the Earth and your connection to the rest of humanity, then you are an Earth Citizen. That being said, it stands to reason that an Earth Citizen should act as an Earth Citizen. This means acting not only for the benefit of your immediate community or nation, but for all of humankind. Because it is easy to fall back into the comfortable but limited scope of our immediate environment, I encourage you to do something that will take your activities one or two steps outside your usual sphere of influence. In other words, I recommend taking some action of deliberate global benefit.

I created the One Dollar Enlightenment Project as an example of the simple actions Earth Citizens can take to help create a better society worldwide. It is a simple concept, and just about anyone can participate. The idea is to donate just one dollar per month toward the International Brain Education

Association's (IBREA) cooperative efforts with the United Nations and other nonprofit entities. I believe that through the painless act of donating a single dollar each month, Earth Citizens will be able to redirect, symbolically and literally, their economic power to benefit other Earth Citizens who are normally outside the international circulation of wealth.

A single one dollar bill can mean a lot more than you might think. Even if you have never been to the United States, you can probably picture a dollar in your mind's eye. If not, think of 1,000 won, 100 yen, a euro, a pound note, or any other type of basic paper currency unit you carry in your wallet. Imagine a brand-new, freshly printed note, slick and crisp to the touch. You can hear it crinkle beneath your fingertips as you run your fingers along its surface. Perhaps you can even smell the printer's ink and the freshly cut paper.

Now, think of an old one-dollar bill, maybe five or ten years old. You can imagine how different it has become. Its texture is now soft and pliable, having passed through the hands of many people on its journey. It might be a bit gray, having picked up its share of grease and grime along the way. Maybe it is slightly ripped or marked with someone's handwriting. From the time this dollar rolled off the printing press, it has humbly played its part in the cultural dance of economic exchange.

But how often do you stop to think how you spend a single dollar? Chances are, you hardly give it a second thought. Oh, you might give a fifty- or even a twenty-dollar bill some thought, but for most of us, a single dollar can pass easily in and out of our hands without much consideration. It's easy to think such a small amount is insignificant. But really, the way we choose to spend a single dollar says a lot about who we are and what we believe in.

First of all, consider what a miraculous thing this dollar is. In reality, it is just paper and ink. But of course, we invest it with much more meaning and value than that would suggest. The dollar bill has meaning because we choose to believe in its value. Any currency that is not trusted in the minds of human beings has no value in the world's economy. The value of a dollar rises and falls based on humanity's collective agreement about the trustworthiness of the economic system it represents.

Although dollars can buy us material objects—cars, food, clothes, and the like—dollars are not really material. No one believes that a dollar's value lies in the value of the paper used by the Federal Reserve. Rather, it has symbolic value. Each dollar represents a certain unit of human energy invested to earn it. For some individuals, that energy investment may be in the form of hard physical labor, while for others it may have required only a millisecond of computerized investment savvy.

Regardless of how a dollar was obtained, it always represents a unit of human energy, energy that we have put toward the production of goods or the delivery of services. Thus how we spend our money is also how we spend our energy. Part of that energy is used the same way that human energy has been used since the dawn of humanity—to obtain the basic necessities of human life, such as food, shelter, and clothing. And for many people around the world, this continues to be the main objective of life and the primary use of money in their lives.

You can think of the One Dollar Enlightenment Project as a meditation on what a dollar means to you in your life. You can ask yourself, "What is the true value of money to me? What does it say about my choices and my way of life?" Through this simple awareness, you can realize how powerful you really are. You do not have to be wealthy to realize that each dollar you spend is like a vote, and each time you vote you are making a statement about the kind of world you want to live in. You will easily see you are able to make a better world if you are willing to go one dollar and one step at a time.

As I have stated before, I think this is a very important time to be alive. Now is the time to reevaluate and reform the habitual choices we have made and the world we have created through those choices. The choices you make now matter more than they ever have before. Times are not easy, but they are indeed a great blessing.

Participation in the One Dollar Enlightenment Project symbolizes your determination to make positive, widely beneficial choices with your money. Today, more than 3 billion people live on less than a single dollar a day. Every day, 3,000 children die of starvation and other preventable diseases, 1.2 billion people do not have access to clean drinking water, and 18 million people each year die unnecessarily for reasons related to poverty.

By giving one dollar per month, you are declaring that you are committed to creating a healthy, peaceful way of life for *all* people on Earth. The IBREA Foundation is working directly with the United Nations to help fulfill its Millennium Development Goals, first by reaching out to mothers with AIDS in developing countries. Just a few dollars a day can help provide these women with the education and medication needed to prevent the spread of AIDS to their unborn children. In the future, IBREA Foundation will team up with other organizations that are also acting for the greater good of planet Earth and its people.

To participate, please fill out and return the form included at the end of this appendix, or visit our Web site, www.iearthcitizen.org.

International Brain Education Association (IBREA) Foundation
Educating the World to Realize the Potential of the Human Brain

Mission of IBREA Foundation

IBREA Foundation is a nonprofit 501(c)3 organization whose mission is to educate individuals, communities, and nations to realize the potential of the human brain to bring health, happiness, and peace to all of humanity and the Earth.

IBREA Foundation increases awareness of the brain's potential through education and training, events, research, publications, and partnerships with others, including the United Nations member states and agencies, governments, corporations, nongovernmental organizations, schools, academic institutions, hospitals, and other community organizations.

We believe that Brain Education is our best hope for the Earth and that the human brain is the key to solving the challenges of our global society.

Vision of IBREA Foundation

The vision of IBREA is for Brain Education to be applied by all people around the world, empowering individuals to take positive action to create health, happiness, and peace for the benefit of all humanity and the Earth.

History and Partners

The IBREA Foundation was founded in 2007 by Ilchi Lee and, along with IBREA Korea (founded in 2004) and IBREA Japan (founded in 2007), collaborates with representatives in more than one hundred countries worldwide to disseminate Brain Education.

Activities of IBREA Foundation

In support of its mission and vision, IBREA Foundation currently

- **conducts events and seminars at the United Nations** in partnership with the Korea Institute of Brain Science (KIBS), a nongovernmental organization in consultative status with the United Nations Economic and Social Council (UNESCO).

- **directs projects to raise awareness of global issues and to support the United Nations Millennium Development Goals,** especially in the areas of education, health, and the environment.

- **supports the dissemination of Brain Education around the world** through collaborations with United Nations member states, agencies, and non-governmental organizations.

- **sponsors events to raise public awareness about the potential of the human brain** to create health, happiness, and peace, including the Annual International Brain Education Conference and Brain HSP Olympiad, the Brain Art Festival, and the Aloha Now Earth Citizen Festival.

For more information about the IBREA Foundation, please visit www.ibrea.org.

For more than thirty years, **Ilchi Lee** has worked tirelessly to bring health, happiness, and peace to the world. The Earth Citizen movement is just one of many such efforts. Currently serving as president of the Korea Institute of Brain Science (KIBS) and the International Brain Education Association (IBREA), Lee believes that the human brain is the key to creating a sustainable, harmonious world culture. Thus, he developed the Brain Education System Training (BEST), which seeks to enhance human potential through a variety of mind-body training methods. He is the author of more than thirty books. For more information, please visit www.ilchi.com.

One Dollar Enlightenment Project

APPLICATION FORM

Yes! As an Earth Citizen, I'd like to join the project.

- ✓ I accept unlimited responsibility for the Earth and its citizens.

- ✓ I trust in the ability of human beings to use their brains for health, happiness, and peace.

- ✓ I take action to create a healthy Earth and a peaceful world.

Name			
Gender ☐ Female ☐ Male Age		Occupation	
Street Address			
City	State	Zip	Country
Phone		Business	
E-mail		Fax	

One Dollar Enlightenment:
☐ $1/month (every month) ☐ $12/year (once a year)

To support IBREA:
☐ $10/month (every month) ☐ $120/year (once a year) ☐ $250/year (once a year)
☐ $500/year (once a year) ☐ $1,000/year (once a year) ☐ other ($)

Pay to the order of IBREA Foundation (Do you need a receipt? Over $25 only) Y / N

Paid by ☐ Cash ☐ Check ☐ Mastercard ☐ Visa ☐ Amex ☐ other (   )

Name on the card

Authorizing signature

Card no.

Exp. date   Zip code

Please fax this form to 928-496-2056 or mail to
IBREA at 866 UN Plaza, Suite 479, New York, NY 10017
For more information or to make changes to your donation,
please contact IBREA at info@ibrea.org or 212-319-0848.